All Around the Farm

By Yuriko Nichols
Illustrated by Michelle Mallard

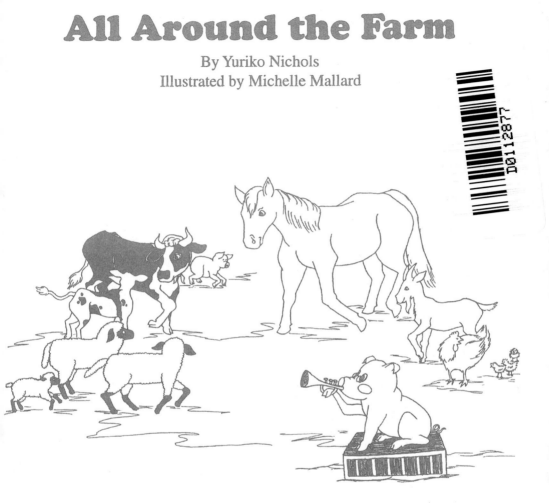

Common Sense Press™

Common Sense Press
8786 Highway 21
Melrose, FL 32666
www.commonsensepress.com

Printed in the United States of America
ISBN 978-1-880892-53-4

Rev 07/09
Printed 08/09

CONTENTS

WILL LITTLE SPARROW FLY?

Little Sparrow fell down from the tree.
Plop! Plop!
Brown Chick said, "You fell! Hee, hee!
Do you think you can fly?"

"Mama Sparrow said I would fly one day.
I have to try and then I will fly,"
said Little Sparrow.

"You are like a chick.
You look like you can fly, but you can not,"
said Brown Chick.

Little Sparrow was sad.

Mama Sparrow said he could fly when it was time.

Now, he did not think he could fly at all.

He sat down.

Drops of tears fell from his face.

Pig sat in the mud.

He could see Little Sparrow.

"Come here, Little Sparrow," Pig said.

"I have a tale to tell you.

In that tree, there was a nest with an egg in it.

In the egg was a very little sparrow.

The little sparrow would try to crack the egg.

Mama Sparrow said he would crack the egg when it was time.

Now, he should rest.

He could try the next day.

Then one day...crack!

He did it!

He made a crack.

That same sparrow would get big one day and fly.

Tell me, Little Sparrow, should you do what Mama Sparrow said?

Should you trust her?

Who was that little sparrow?"

"That sparrow was me," said Little Sparrow.

"When I was very little, I had to wait for the time
to crack the egg.

I could trust Mama Sparrow then,
and I will trust her now."

Little Sparrow did not give up.

He would try and fall down.

Then he would try the next day.

Little Sparrow fell ten times.

Pig was a big help.

He would yell, "Good try, Little Sparrow."

Then one day, Little Sparrow could fly to the top
of the tree.

He could see the trees below him.

Little Sparrow called to Pig,

"How do you like this try?"

"It is time for you to fly, Little Sparrow,"

smiled Pig.

HARD, SHORT HAY

"Do your chore, Son," said Mama Cow.

It was too late.

Mama Cow couldn't see Son at all.

He was playing with a dog.

"I would not let my Son run off if he did not do

his chore," said Goat.

She went to the gate of the stall.

She gave Mama Cow a sharp look.

Mama Cow had a plan.

She would not do his chore.

"Son must do his chore."

Son came to the barn for lunch.

Mama Cow said, "Do your chore, Son."

"Why? If I make a hay bed now, I will just have to make the hay bed again. Why not let the hay bed stay the same?" asked Son.

Mama Cow spoke to Son in a nice way. "The hay is now hard and short. You will not sleep well in a bed of hard, short hay. It smells, too."

"It is O.K. I can sleep in hard, short hay. Now, I want to go play with the dog," said Son.

He ran to the yard.

Goat gave Mama Cow another sharp look.
Goat said, "I will not live in a barn with such a
bad smell."
Mama Cow gave her a smile.

She was a smart mama.

The sun went down.

Son was ready for sleep.

He was glad that he did not have to make the hay bed.

But the hay bed was hard.

The short hay was poking him.

The hay bed had a bad smell, too.

Mama Cow went to sleep.

But Son could not sleep.

When the sun came up, Mama Cow woke up.

Son was quick to make his hay bed.

Mama Cow spoke in a kind way.

"Why do you do that, Son?

You will just have to make the hay bed again."

"I will be glad to make my hay bed each day.

Then I can sleep.

Hard, short hay does not make a good bed," said

Son with a smile.

HOUND DOG TAKES THE JOB

Mouse ran out of the house.

He ran around the yard.

He ran into the barn.

He stopped when he found some straw and corn.

He ate and ate some more.

"The mice are eating all the straw and corn.

The mice get fat, and I get thin," moaned Horse.

He made a loud sound to arouse Cat.

Cat opened one eye.

With a yawn, she lifted a paw.

"Hush, Horse, I am dreaming about my life in the big town.

I do not belong on the farm," she pouted.

Horse spoke to all the animals in the barn.
"Cat does not keep the mice away.
Who will take her job?"

"Not I," said Cow.
"Not I," said Hen.
"Not I," said Goat.

Hound Dog came into the barn.
"I can keep the mice far away from the farm."

"What? You can not even keep the fleas away!"
shouted Goat.
All the animals howled.

Pig did not howl.
"Wait. We must let
Hound Dog have a
chance."

The animals agreed.
That day, Hound Dog
did not sleep.
He kept the mice away.
There was not a mouse
to be found.

When he saw a mouse, he chased it far away from the barn.

Hound Dog's loud growl made the mice afraid to come back.

All week, Hound Dog kept the mice away.

One day, he could hear the barn animals speaking.

"He is a fine dog," said Cow.

"What a dog!" said Hen.

"He is the best dog," said Goat.

Hound Dog smiled from ear to ear.
He was proud to be a hound dog.

CAT VISITS THE TOWN

Cat sent a letter to Prissy Cat.

The letter said,

"It is urgent that I visit you.

I must depart from farm life."

Cat waited at her door.

At last, Cat got a letter back from Prissy.

Prissy said to come visit now.

Cat made some firm plans.

She would leave on the first bus to town.

Cat met Prissy on the corner of Main and Third Street.

The town was crowded.

She found Prissy waiting under a tall fir tree.

"How nice to see you," said Cat.

Prissy grabbed her arm.
She said, "My curls are falling,
and my feet are hurting.
Let's hurry and go home."

They drove up to a beautiful house.
Cat said, "Wow, this is better than my house at
the farm."

"Sh...you must be still," said Prissy.
"We must wait until the
dogs are asleep."

"Why can't we go
inside the house?"
asked Cat.

"You silly cat.
I do not live *inside* the house.
I live under the porch," said Prissy.

"I see," said Cat. She was surprised.
"Where do you sleep?"

"I sleep in the ferns under the porch,"
said Prissy.

"I see," said Cat. She was surprised again.
"What do you eat?"

"I eat things from the trash
the man throws away," said Prissy.

"I see," said Cat. She was very surprised.
"Just one more thing," said Cat.

"What?" asked Prissy.

"Why must we wait until the dogs are asleep?"

Just then, the dogs growled. "Arf, arf, arf!"

The cats ran around the curve.

The dogs were coming fast.

Cat saw the road that leads to the farm.

She turned the other way and saw the dogs.

Cat waved to Prissy.

Prissy saw Cat running all the way home.

Cat returned with dirt on her face.

She ran in the door.

She sat on the couch and lifted her feet.

"I am so glad to be home.

My feet hurt, but my nerves feel better."

CAT WAS WRONG

Cat returned to the farm very sad.

She could not be a town cat, and she lost her job on the farm.

"I guess I do not have a job now."

What could she do now?

Could she find a new job here?

No! Every farm cat chases mice.

That is all they do well.

Cat sat down and started to sob.

"I was wrong.

I *am* a farm cat.

I love the farm," she said to herself.

Pig sat in the mud.
He said, "Why don't
you tell all the
animals that?"

Cat looked at Pig.

She started a loud cry.

"I guess they will make fun of me if I do that."

"A few of them may, but most want you here,"
said Pig.

So when the sun came up, Pig blew the horn and called the animals to his pen.

"Guess what? Cat is here.

She wants to tell you something."

"I was wrong about the town.

I was wrong to leave the farm.

I love it here. I am sorry I quit my job.

Will you forgive me?" Cat said.

Mama Cow spoke first, "I will forgive you.

I missed you, Cat.

I am glad you

are back."

Cat looked up at the animals.

She saw a few harsh looks but more smiles.

Cat gave them a smile.

But she had one concern.

"What will we tell Hound Dog?"

Just then, Hound Dog jumped out of the barn.

"Cat, you are back! Hurray!"

Hound Dog saw Son and said, "Let's play.

I will race you to the big oak tree."

Off they ran.

Hound Dog made happy barks all the way to

the tree.

Cat could hear a mouse chew on some corn.
She jumped up and chased the mouse far, far
away.

THE BEST WORK IN THE WORLD

Hurray! Cat has returned.

There was a big party.

Everyone was shouting.

Hound Dog was glad Cat was back, too.

"Cat always did belong on the farm," he said proudly.

Hound Dog was happy, but he had a worry.

"What work will I do now?"

Pig saw Hound Dog's concern.

He gathered all the animals for a short meeting.

As always, Pig blew the horn to start the barn meeting.

"This is the word.

We are all glad that Cat has returned.

But now Hound Dog

has no work.

Hound Dog is

worthy of

our help.

We must think

of a plan."

The next morning, Farmer came into the barn.
Cow said, "Hound Dog is a good worker."
Farmer just listened.

Then Farmer led Goat out to the barnyard.
Goat said, "Farmer, Hound Dog did a good job

with the mice."
Farmer just listened.

The chickens said,
"Hound Dog does not
look like much on the
outside, but he is a
smart dog."
Farmer just listened.

Farmer looked for Hound Dog
and found him curled up in the yard.

"Hound Dog, I need someone to herd my sheep.
It is hard work, but I think you can do it."

Hound Dog bounded up the hill with Farmer.
He barked and made the sheep hurry up.
Hound Dog stayed with the herd until dark.

Farmer patted Hound Dog.

He said, "You are a smart sheep dog."

Hound Dog smiled at his owner.

"It is hard work, but it is the best work in the world."